This book is dedicated to all the young people
I've had the opportunity to meet and work with.
Thank you for inspiring me every day with
your curiosity, kindness, and resilience!

CONTENTS

EMPATHY FOR KIDS

EMPATHY
for Kids

30 Fun Activities to Foster Emotional Awareness, Compassion, and Kindness

NICOLE TOLENTINO, LCSW, MSW

Illustrated by Denise Holmes

ROCKRIDGE
PRESS

For general information on our other products and services or to obtain technical support, please contact our Customer Care Department within the United States at (866) 744-2665, or outside the United States at (510) 253-0500.

Rockridge Press publishes its books in a variety of electronic and print formats. Some content that appears in print may not be available in electronic books, and vice versa.

TRADEMARKS: Rockridge Press and the Rockridge Press logo are trademarks or registered trademarks of Callisto Media Inc. and/or its affiliates, in the United States and other countries, and may not be used without written permission. All other trademarks are the property of their respective owners. Rockridge Press is not associated with any product or vendor mentioned in this book.

Interior and Cover Designer: Irene Vandervoort
Art Producer: Maya Melenchuk
Editor: Laura Bryn Sisson
Production Editor: Jael Fogle
Production Manager: Jose Olivera

Illustration © 2022 Denise Holmes

Paperback ISBN: 978-1-63878-124-0 | eBook ISBN: 978-1-63878-761-7
R0

INTRODUCTION

Welcome caregivers, educators, and all other adults! My name is Nicole, and I am a licensed clinical social worker. I have been teaching and learning with children since I was a young person myself—from studying early childhood education in college to my professional career working as an outpatient therapist and school social worker, and even to my summers working in adventure therapy! Through these endeavors, it has become my passion to help young people build their self-awareness and social-emotional skills so that they may be better equipped to overcome life's challenges.

Building successful interpersonal relationships and identifying emotions are two of the most important skills children can learn. Empathetic children go on to establish more fulfilling relationships and create a positive impact in their communities. They are also more likely to take on leadership roles.

If teaching empathy to children seems difficult to you, you're not alone! When I first started working with young people in this area, it appeared complicated and hard to grasp. But after some practice and lots of activities, my clients and students excelled. They were soon able to put themselves in others' shoes and solve problems in an empathetic way. It was inspiring!

The goal of this book is to help you guide your child's growth in social-emotional development and compassion. They will learn ways to identify emotions in themselves and others, recognize the impact of their actions, and develop the skill of empathy. It is my hope that in working through these activities with children, you will create a space for quality time together and continue to build a positive foundation for years to come!

CHAPTER ONE

Teaching Empathy to Little Ones

Children come into this world with an intuitive sense of joy, curiosity, and creativity. From the moment they are born, little ones are actively exploring their surroundings and learning to navigate through a world of relationships and interactions with others. Eventually, young children begin to develop the basic skills needed to understand themselves and empathize with those around them. Empathy plays a key role in creating the foundation for a child's social-emotional intelligence. This chapter is meant to provide caregivers with a quick guide to understanding empathy and what this skill may look like for your little one.

What Is Empathy?

Empathy is the ability to understand and share the feelings of another person and to see a situation from someone else's point of view. According to Daniel Goleman, renowned psychologist and author of the book *Emotional Intelligence*, there are three different types of empathy: cognitive, emotional, and compassionate. Each form of empathy plays its own role in understanding and connecting with others.

* **Cognitive:** The ability to be aware of someone else's perspective. A person can understand what another may be feeling in an intellectual way, without necessarily sympathizing with the other person's emotions.

* **Emotional:** The capability to feel what someone else is feeling, as if the emotion were contagious. An example is when a child cries in response to hearing another child's cry.

* **Compassionate:** Being able to understand another's feelings and then choose to take action to help them solve a problem or provide support. This type involves the ability to guess what another person may need to feel better.

Why Empathy Is Important

Empathy is a skill that can be learned at any time in life, from young children just beginning their adventure to those in later phases of life. People who are taught empathy at an early age can often build stronger relationships and develop a greater sense of self. With practice in identifying and responding to emotions, children can begin to build the foundation of empathy.

Benefits of Empathy

Showing empathy toward others allows children to cultivate stronger social connections and build lasting relationships. Children with this skill are able to regulate their own emotions more easily and identify the emotions of others.

Empathetic children are often able to prevent bullying and encourage tolerance. Later in life, having empathetic skills allows adults to achieve greater personal and professional success as well as maintain strong interpersonal relationships. The ability to be perceptive also plays a critical role in being an effective leader.

The Importance of Sincerity

Sometimes adults will force children to use empathetic language, such as saying "I'm sorry" when interacting with others in situations where they do not actually feel sorry or understand what they have done wrong. Pressuring children to use empathetic language without understanding the reason will not help them to learn empathetic behavior. In fact, it may deter them from building the curiosity to understand what others may be feeling. Parents and caregivers can help their little ones cultivate an understanding of other people's emotions by asking open-ended questions, such as "How do you think they're feeling?" or "What can you do to help?"

Building Blocks of Empathy

By the age of five, most children have already made great strides in forming their emotional intelligence. They have begun to recognize their individuality and can see that others operate in different ways with their own set of emotions, thoughts, and feelings. Many children are even able to envision what type of response may be comforting or helpful to others in a given situation.

There are five main aspects of empathy that we will focus on in this book:

* Building awareness of our own emotions

* Recognizing and understanding the emotions of others

* Seeing other people's perspectives

* Acting out of compassion

* Expanding our circles of concern

Each of these areas is essential in establishing empathetic skills. Understanding how each emotion looks and feels builds the foundation of empathy, and being able to see other people's perspectives continues this process. By putting ourselves in someone else's shoes, we can identify compassionate actions and responses to help others.

Three-Year-Olds

At three years old, a child's social and emotional awareness is still in the early stages. These little ones are a bit self-centered and are just beginning to understand their own feelings. Because identifying and regulating their emotions is still new, they have little control over them and may act on impulse. They will typically progress socially by showing more interest in trying new things as well as advancing from playing *near* other children to playing *with* them.

CAPABILITIES AND LIMITATIONS

Little ones in this age group are typically able to understand what feelings are and what they can look like. They may also realize that other people have their own feelings. Often their needs will overrule the needs of others. They can show affection toward peers without being told. Most three-year-old children can follow simple directions and have short back-and-forth conversations using the basic rules of grammar. Their attention span lasts about 5 to 10 minutes. Children of this age may become upset with major changes in their routine or if their needs are not met immediately. This is where practicing their emotion identification and regulation can be helpful.

THE EMPATHETIC THREE-YEAR-OLD

Many three-year-olds can comprehend a connection between emotions and desires. If they want to build a tower of blocks, they understand that they will be happy when they build it and angry if it is knocked down. If a child can relate someone else's situation to their own experience, they can typically respond to their emotions and offer simple gestures of support.

Four-Year-Olds

By age four, many little ones can display a higher level of emotional knowledge. They start to build more meaningful friendships with peers and spend more time talking about what interests them. They can hold longer conversations with those around them and respond to others with authenticity. Their understanding and care of other people's feelings becomes more prominent, and they can begin focusing on the effects of their words and actions.

CAPABILITIES AND LIMITATIONS

Most children of this age make up their own games with unique rules and objectives. They will engage in dramatic play by acting out situations they have seen at home, such as cooking in the kitchen or going to the grocery store. They can take turns while playing cooperatively with peers and enjoy making others laugh, forming the beginnings of their sense of humor. Their attention span is about 10 to 15 minutes, but they are more likely to stay engaged if they feel comfortable and successful in an activity. Children of this age also become more independent in daily tasks, such as choosing what clothes to wear.

THE EMPATHETIC FOUR-YEAR-OLD

Four-year-olds can often respond to other people's feelings in an emotional way as well as a cognitive way. They can see when someone else is upset, empathize with them, and then identify potential solutions or supportive behaviors that can be helpful to the other person.

Five-Year-Olds

By age five, many children begin to shift focus away from themselves and toward the collective. Young people at this age tend to jump back and forth between prioritizing themselves and pleasing their friends. They want to be liked by peers and caregivers. They express emotions verbally instead of in a physical way—by stating wants and needs instead of hitting or grabbing. They can better identify emotions in themselves and then find the words to express these emotions to others.

CAPABILITIES AND LIMITATIONS

Five-year-olds have the skills to carry on longer conversations, recalling words and concepts from their growing vocabulary. They can understand the rules of different games and enjoy playing collaboratively with friends. Awareness of moral reasoning grows and children start to recognize the difference between right and wrong. Their attention span has increased to 12 to 20 minutes. Most children can ignore minor distractions outside of their immediate task and will continue to stay motivated if an activity is related to their personal interests. They may also be able to stick to frustrating tasks longer because of an increase in emotional regulation skills. Because many of these self-regulation skills are still a work in progress, there can be sudden changes in attitude, where children go from being cooperative to being demanding relatively quickly.

THE EMPATHETIC FIVE-YEAR-OLD

Five-year-olds are often more in tune with their own feelings, which allows them to identify the feelings of others more accurately. They care about their loved ones and want them to feel safe and happy. These little ones use their capacity for observing nonverbal cues to help put their empathetic skills into practice.

Every Child Is Beautifully Different

Although there are milestones in childhood development, each child progresses at their own pace with their own unique set of strengths and challenges. Temperament and physical development, along with an array of outside factors, play a role in the progress of social-emotional advancement. The activities in this book can be adapted to meet the needs of children at any stage in their social-emotional journey.

There are a number of common challenges that may arise in the development of preschool-aged children. Some of these may be related to developmental delays, autism spectrum disorder, cognitive and physical disabilities, or a variety of other social-emotional obstacles. For children who have any of these challenges, attempting to engage in modified versions of the following activities can be helpful. Sometimes a simple conversation or repeated opportunities to model skills can assist a child in making progress.

If a child has a shorter attention span than their peers, you may be able to engage in an activity by splitting it into multiple sessions or allowing short breaks throughout. This will create space for your child to recharge and avoid feeling overwhelmed. Another helpful modification may be to center the activity around your child's individual interests. For example, if your child loves superheroes, many of the activities can be adapted to include pictures or scenarios involving characters they like. Presenting young people with a choice, such as completing one activity over another, may also help.

Modeling Empathy

A helpful tool in a child's journey of learning and practicing empathy is repeated opportunities to observe empathetic behavior by adults in daily life. Empathetic behavior must be consistently modeled by adults and encouraged in children before it can become part of their instinctive behavior. When adults model empathy, children are more likely to establish a secure attachment to the adults in their lives. Little ones who are securely attached to their adult caregivers feel safe and loved, which in turn leads to an ability to be more sensitive toward other people's emotional needs.

Another key aspect to keep in mind when teaching a child empathy is the idea of co-regulation. Co-regulation can be defined as warm and responsive interactions that provide the support and modeling children need to understand, express, and modulate their thoughts, feelings, and behaviors (Murray et al. 2015). An example of this would be responding to an upset child by speaking to them in a calm, soothing tone. This action encourages the upset child to bring their own emotions to a level that matches yours. Learning how to regulate one's emotions can be very difficult at first, but through co-regulation, children can practice this skill by collaborating with a trusted adult.

SAFETY TIPS

As with any other activities involving sharp objects, small pieces, and art supplies, please be careful! Note any hazardous objects or materials during the activity to encourage the safety of your child. Remember to use child-friendly paints and markers. It may be helpful to place any small pieces, such as beads or sequins, in containers to ensure that they are not lost or ingested. Be sure that children are always in your line of sight during the activities or that they are supervised by a responsible adult. If using a hot glue gun for any of the creative projects, please be sure to only allow adult use and keep out of reach of young children. Children should use age-appropriate safety scissors while participating in any crafting activities.

How to Use This Book

This book is meant to be used as a source of ideas for encouraging and guiding children in empathy-building exercises. Each chapter builds upon the skills learned in the previous chapter. It may be helpful to complete activities in order, but it is completely up to you and your child which activities you'd like to try. You know your child's unique abilities and interests best! Each activity includes:

* A messiness rating on a scale of 0 (not messy at all) to 4 (the messiest)

* An estimated preparation time

* An estimated activity time

* Appropriate age

* A list of materials

* The activity steps

* A helpful tip

All the activities included in this book are designed with you in mind. They have been constructed to be quick and require very little prep work or cleanup. Some activities can even be implemented throughout the day, such as at bedtime or on the drive home from school with no materials necessary. Use the ideas presented in this book as an opportunity to bond with your child and display your own authenticity. Being engaged and genuinely excited to participate in exercises with your child can help invigorate your little one's interest in learning and growing alongside you!

CHAPTER TWO

Your Feelings

This chapter is all about how to help little ones increase awareness of their own emotions. Through guided activities, they will practice identifying and understanding their feelings. Building a child's competence in emotion identification and regulation allows them to be more in control of their behaviors. This prepares young people to stop and think before they react to a situation and to ask what they or others may need.

BEACH BALL FEELINGS

This activity allows children to focus inward and name their current feelings or remember a time when they felt a specific emotion. Practicing how to identify emotions can strengthen self-awareness.

MATERIALS:

COLORFUL BEACH BALL

PERMANENT MARKER

STEPS:

1. Inside each color block on a beach ball, write a different emotion word, such as *happy*, *sad*, or *angry*, along with a face representing that emotion. In one of the color blocks, write "I feel _____."

2. Tell children that once they catch the ball to share a time that they felt the emotion shown in the color block that their left-hand thumb is touching (younger children may need assistance with this part). If their thumb is touching the color block with the open-ended sentence, the child should share how they feel right now.

3. Take turns tossing the beach ball back and forth with children.

AGE ADAPTATION: For older children who may have a more advanced emotional vocabulary, include more difficult feeling words, such as *jealous*, *frustrated*, or *embarrassed*. For younger children, skip writing out the words, and just use faces, with a question mark for the open-ended sentence.

MIX-AND-MATCH EGGS

Being able to imagine and create facial expressions can be a great way to start interpreting different aspects of visual emotions.

MATERIALS:

PLASTIC EGG HALVES THAT FIT TOGETHER (10 EGGS)

PERMANENT MARKER

STEPS:

1. Draw a face on each egg—eyes with eyebrows on the tops and mouths on the bottoms. Make sure that each egg is showing a different expression.

2. Encourage children to name the emotions of each egg and then allow them time to play with the egg halves, mixing them up and creating their own face pairings. Once they have created a new face, ask, "How is that egg feeling?"

3. After a few minutes, prompt children to create specific facial expressions, such as happy, sad, confused, etc.

SIMPLE SWAP: If you do not have access to plastic eggs, this activity can be created on pieces of paper with faces on them instead. Children can also practice making faces with other materials, such as magnets or paper cutouts of eyes, noses, and mouths.

HOPPING INTO FEELINGS

This interactive game will help children practice identifying emotion words. Repeatedly recalling the names of emotions and what they feel like can help little ones build a strong emotional vocabulary.

MATERIALS:

SIDEWALK CHALK

STEPS:

1. Find a paved surface outside and draw 5 to 10 boxes with chalk on the ground.

2. Inside each box, write an emotion word along with a face depicting that emotion. Get creative by drawing different shapes or including hopscotch-like designs between each emotion word.

3. Say one emotion and invite children to hop into the corresponding box. Encourage further engagement by asking when a person may feel that emotion, or prompt children by saying phrases like "Jump to the emotion that someone would feel if they got a new puppy."

4. Repeat with all the emotion words listed in the boxes.

SIMPLE SWAP: If more than one child is participating, have children toss a beanbag into the boxes instead of jumping in. They can also race to see who can identify the correct answer first.

EMOTIONS IN THE BODY

Associating emotions with how they physically feel in the body can help a child be more connected to themselves. Giving children an opportunity to think about where in their bodies they feel different emotions can help children identify those emotions more easily.

MATERIALS:

PAPER

COLORING UTENSILS

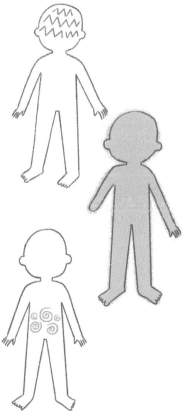

STEPS:

1. Draw a simple person outline on a sheet of paper and write an emotion word underneath.

2. Ask children to color in the body to show how that emotion feels. Invite them to think about where they feel this emotion in the body and what that may look or feel like—is it a twisting pain, a tight squeeze, a fuzzy warm feeling?

3. Repeat this activity as many times as you'd like with different emotion words.

AGE ADAPTATION: For younger ones, simply identifying what color each emotion feels like (and why) can be a helpful exercise. Ask children to fill each body shape with the color(s) that emotion makes them think of.

MESSINESS:	PREP TIME:	ACTIVITY TIME:	AGE:
1	10 minutes	15 minutes	4 to 5

FEELINGS CARD MATCH

This game allows little ones to practice their emotion identification skills while also improving concentration and training visual memory.

MATERIALS:

SCISSORS

PAPER OR CARDSTOCK

MARKERS

STEPS:

1. Use scissors to cut out 10 to 20 equal-shaped cards from the paper.

2. Write an emotion word on one card and draw a picture depicting that emotion on another card so the word and picture appear on separate cards that make a matching pair. Repeat with different emotions until all the cards are full.

3. Mix up the cards and lay them on a flat surface, facedown between you and your child.

4. Take turns picking two cards from the group. If they match, the player gets to keep the pair and continue picking two cards until they choose two that do not match. Play until there are no cards left.

5. The player with the most pairs wins the game.

AGE ADAPTATION: For older children, include a higher number of cards with more advanced feeling words on them. Prompt your child to share a time when they have felt the emotion on the card.

MESSINESS:	PREP TIME:	ACTIVITY TIME:	AGE:
0	None	5 minutes	4 to 5

FIVE-FINGER BREATHING

Children's ability to regulate their emotions and calm uncomfortable feelings can help create space for empathy toward others. It allows a child to pause and respond to those around them instead of potentially reacting impulsively.

MATERIALS:

NONE

STEPS:

1. Instruct your child to hold their left hand out in front of them, palm facing inward.

2. Have them use their right pointer finger to slowly trace up and down each finger on the left hand, as if they were tracing their hand on paper.

3. Say, "As you move up each finger, take a slow breath in. When you move down each finger, slowly breathe out."

4. Practice tracing all five fingers a few times.

5. The next time your child is upset or appears to be experiencing strong negative emotions, remind them of their new skill of five-finger breathing.

GET CREATIVE: Deep breathing can be facilitated in many ways. Tracing a square, triangle, or figure eight while inhaling and exhaling slowly is another great way to guide calming breaths.

CHAPTER THREE

Other People's Feelings

This chapter is about children learning to observe, understand, and care about the feelings of others. Once little ones are connected to their own feelings, they can begin exploring the feelings of those around them. Verbal and nonverbal cues, such as reading facial expressions, tone of voice, and body language, are all tools used to decode how others feel. By learning how to identify these signals, young people will develop the skills they need to put themselves in other people's shoes.

MESSINESS:	PREP TIME:	ACTIVITY TIME:	AGE:
0	5 minutes	15 to 20 minutes	5

EMOTIONS CHARADES

Being able to identify emotions and what they look like is an important step to understanding what these emotions feel like. By acting out each emotion word and connecting these words to facial expressions and behaviors, children will be able to identify these feelings more readily in themselves and others.

MATERIALS:

PENCIL

5 TO 10 SMALL PIECES OF PAPER

BOWL

STEPS:

1. Write one emotion word with a face depicting that emotion on each piece of paper, fold it, and place it into the bowl.

2. Take turns picking from the bowl and acting out the emotion using facial expressions, sounds, and actions while the other player guesses which emotion is being acted out.

3. Take time after each turn to reflect on how the emotion was identified (body language, words used, facial expressions, etc.).

GET CREATIVE: To make things a little more difficult, try playing the game with facial expressions only!

SCOUTING BODY LANGUAGE

Reading body language is an essential part of communicating with others. It helps us interpret what someone's words really mean and how they are feeling at a given moment. Learning to read these nonverbal messages can help children understand which actions to take to show empathy toward others.

MATERIALS:

PRINTOUTS OR PAPER

STEPS:

1. Print out an emotions chart from the internet, or write down a list of emotions on a piece of paper. (See Resources on page 51 for a link to an emotions chart.)

2. Take a walk with your little one in a place where there are other people around for an emotions scavenger hunt.

3. As you walk, see how many emotions from your chart you can find among the people around you. Discuss their body language, such as posture, eye movement, use of space, and facial expressions. Check off each emotion as you find it.

GET CREATIVE: Discuss with your child why they think a person is showing a particular emotion. Ask, "What do you think that person is feeling? If you were standing, sitting, or walking that way, what do you think you would want or need?"

TRANSLATING FACES

Facial expressions are one of the most universal forms of body language and a useful tool in reading other people's emotions.

MATERIALS:

MAGAZINES

SAFETY SCISSORS

BOWL

STEPS:

1. Look through a magazine together and cut out faces that show emotion.

2. Put the collection in a bowl and have children pick a face at random.

3. Ask children to study each facial expression and say what that person is feeling and why.

4. You can also ask questions like "What is their mouth doing?" or "Are their eyebrows relaxed or scrunched?"

AGE ADAPTATION: Sit in front of a mirror with younger children and make various facial expressions yourself. Invite children to copy your expressions and ask them what emotion you are showing. This can help little ones understand how the different parts of the face come together to show an emotion.

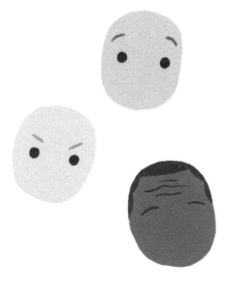

INTERPRETING TONE OF VOICE

Tone of voice, which includes volume and inflection, plays an influential role in expressing our emotions. This verbal cue tells others how we are feeling and adds to the full picture of a person's emotional state.

MATERIALS:

NONE

STEPS:

1. Think of a neutral phrase, such as "The boy walked slowly over the bridge."

2. Ask your child to listen carefully, then recite this phrase to them multiple times. Each time, have a specific emotion in mind and create a different tone of voice.

3. After each recitation, ask your child which emotion they believe you are expressing.

4. Once they get the hang of the game, have your child try reciting a phrase for you.

GET CREATIVE: Make this activity more challenging by adding body language and facial expressions that either do or do not match with your tone. Ask your child what emotion each type of communication is showing (such as tone of voice vs. body/facial language), and whether they match or conflict.

IN THEIR SHOES

Taking on the perspective of our favorite movie or TV show characters can be the first step in practicing to walk in someone else's shoes. We can see the events leading up to a situation and can often imagine what the characters on the screen may be thinking or feeling.

MATERIALS:

ANY TYPE OF CHILD-APPROPRIATE VIDEO (TV SHOW, MOVIE, CARTOON)

STEPS:

1. Put on a video that the children like.

2. Every so often, pause the video and ask children questions about what each character on the screen may be thinking or feeling.

3. Ask children what they notice about the character's body language or facial expressions.

SIMPLE SWAP: This activity can be done easily with books as well. Take time to pause while reading a picture book to reflect on the questions in the activity. Practicing these skills often will help build children's capacity to understand the perspective of others.

EMOTION STORYBOARD

During this activity, little ones will have the opportunity to use their imagination and draw scenes of themselves or others experiencing different emotions. This can be done in boxes, where the parts of the story progress through each box. The storyboards can include events leading up to an emotion and the aftermath.

MATERIALS:

DRAWING UTENSILS

PAPER

STEPS:

1. Draw three large boxes in a row on a piece of paper.

2. Invite children to draw a scenario in which a person feels a particular emotion. Draw each step of the story in a different box. The first box can show what leads to the emotion. The second box can show the character feeling the emotion. The third box can show what happens next.

3. Have children share their stories afterward.

GET CREATIVE: Once the storyboard is complete, encourage children to act out their stories. This could include asking for help from a couple of friends to play different parts, or it can be a solo show! Acting out these scenarios is great practice for taking on other people's perspectives.

CHAPTER FOUR

Someone Else's Shoes

This chapter is all about learning to see things from another person's perspective. Perceiving a situation or event from someone else's point of view is a useful skill that helps children understand what a person may need in a particular moment. By learning to imagine how others may be feeling, children will begin to develop the tools they need to act or react with kindness and compassion for those around them.

PUPPET ROLE-PLAY

Role-playing provides children with an opportunity to express themselves in a safe space. They can make suggestions and share ideas comfortably through the puppet instead of themselves. This creates a space for children to play out scenes and situations that may reflect their own experiences.

MATERIALS:

PUPPETS OR STUFFED ANIMALS

STEPS:

1. Use puppets or stuffed animals to start a conversation with your little one. Take turns suggesting ideas for scenes to act out.

2. Guide children's play by encouraging empathetic behavior. Make comments like "The bear seems angry—he's stomping his feet and his face is red" or ask questions like "What do you think Dolly wants to do?"

3. Be sure to model compassionate responses for children and emphasize kind actions through the role-play scenarios.

GET CREATIVE: Design your own puppets with your child using paper bags, markers, and other crafting materials. Design each puppet with a different facial expression, showing various emotions. Take turns using each puppet with your child and see what types of situations appear.

MESSINESS:	PREP TIME:	ACTIVITY TIME:	AGE:
1	2 minutes	10 to 15 minutes	3 to 4

SAME OR DIFFERENT?

This activity will help children understand that different people can have diverse perspectives. It is useful to acknowledge that sometimes others share your opinion and sometimes they do not.

MATERIALS:

PAPER

MARKERS

STEPS:

1. Distribute pieces of paper so that you and your child each have about 5 pieces each.

2. Think of questions that often lead people to give a range of answers, such as "What is your favorite ice-cream flavor?" or "Do you like summer or fall better?"

3. Present one question to your child and ask them to draw a picture of their answer. Meanwhile, draw your own answer.

4. Share your answers and reasons behind them. Reflect on whether your answers were the same or different.

5. Repeat at least 5 times.

6. Talk about how people can have the same or different opinions about things. Ask, "What would the world be like if everyone had the same opinions?"

AGE ADAPTATION: For younger children, this activity can be done in the form of a conversation. Discuss your child's favorites and share yours. Make note that they are not always the same.

IF I WERE YOU

This activity allows children to put themselves into other people's shoes and imagine how that person may respond or feel in different situations.

MATERIALS:

PAPER

SCISSORS

PENCIL

STEPS:

1. Think of 3 to 5 problem-solving scenarios that your child could potentially encounter, such as "someone is using the pencil you want to use" or "another child at the park says something mean to you."

2. Cut out 5 to 10 playing card-size rectangles from the paper. With your child's help, write down the names of different people they know well, such as yourself, a grandparent, a sibling, or a friend.

3. Share one of your prepared scenarios with your child, then ask them to draw a card from the deck. Invite your child to share how they would respond to the problem if they were the person on the card.

4. Repeat with various scenarios, drawing a different card for each.

GET CREATIVE: Encourage your child to get involved by asking them to provide names of other important people in their lives or sharing their thoughts about situations that they have experienced already.

MESSINESS:	PREP TIME:	ACTIVITY TIME:	AGE:
0	5 minutes	10 minutes	4 to 5

REVERSIBLE FIGURES

Looking at reversible figures and discussing how two different images can exist at the same time helps children understand how differing viewpoints can also exist together.

MATERIALS:

REVERSIBLE FIGURE PRINTOUTS (SUCH AS THE ONE PICTURED BELOW)

STEPS:

1. Search online for reversible figures and print out a few examples. (See Resources on page 51 for a link to reversible figures.)

2. Show children one of the figures and ask them what they see.

3. If children have difficulty seeing an image, point out aspects of one of the images until they are able to see it.

4. Once children can see one side of the figure, guide them toward being able to see the other one.

5. Repeat this action with each reversible figure printout.

6. Discuss how different people have different points of view of the same picture. Relate the activity to the way people can see different sides to the same story, or take on differing perspectives of a situation.

SIMPLE SWAP: This activity can also be done viewing clouds in the sky or ink blots. Ask your child what images and figures they see and share what you see from your perspective.

BLINDFOLDED OBSTACLE COURSE

During this activity, children will take on the perspective of two different roles. They will also learn about the effect that our words and actions can have on others.

MATERIALS:

OBJECTS FROM AROUND THE HOUSE TO BE USED AS OBSTACLES, SUCH AS JUMP ROPE, BROOM, CHAIRS, ETC.

BLINDFOLD

STEPS:

1. Set out an obstacle course using objects from around the house—things to walk around, under, or over.

2. Blindfold your child and then tell them that you will be helping them to get through the course with guiding instructions, such as "Take two steps toward me, now five steps straight ahead."

3. Once your child has gotten to the end of the course, reflect together on how it felt to be in each role and about the challenges that you both faced.

4. Switch roles and allow your child to provide you with directions to get through the course.

5. Ask your little one what it was like to be in the other position. Talk about how clear directions made the activity easier, and relate this to how it's easier to get along when we communicate effectively with others.

SIMPLE SWAP: If your child does not feel comfortable being blindfolded, this activity can be done with eyes open.

WHAT WOULD YOU DO?

In this activity, children are encouraged to invent their own plans for how they would handle a situation. They can then reflect on how their response could affect others.

MATERIALS:

PAPER

COLORING UTENSILS

STEPS:

1. Think of a few scenarios in which someone could exhibit empathy. For example, "You see your friend fall and get hurt—what would you do?" or "A little boy just lost his dog—how could you help him?"

2. Share each scenario with children and ask them to draw a picture of what they would do in that situation.

3. Invite children to share their picture with you. Ask follow-up questions about how they arrived at that decision, or how their chosen action may affect those around them.

SIMPLE SWAP: For children who do not enjoy drawing pictures, this activity can be acted out in role-play. Use props to make it even more fun!

CHAPTER FIVE

You Can Help, Too!

This chapter is about children learning how to respond to other people's emotions as well as how to act with kindness and compassion toward others. Taking initiative to help others feel supported and cared for builds compassion. By learning how to respond with consideration toward others, little ones can develop tools that will help them extend empathy toward those outside of their inner circle.

MESSINESS:	PREP TIME:	ACTIVITY TIME:	AGE:
2	2 minutes	10 to 15 minutes	3 to 5

KINDNESS CARDS

Reaching out to friends or family members and offering a symbol of kindness can help increase children's empathy and compassion. Helping to make someone else's day better gives children the chance to feel proud of themselves and their impact on other people.

MATERIALS:

PAPER

SCISSORS (OPTIONAL)

CRAFTING MATERIALS, SUCH AS COLORING UTENSILS, MARKERS, STICKERS, GLITTER GLUE, ETC.

ENVELOPE

PEN

POSTAGE STAMP

STEPS:

1. Invite children to think of at least one friend or relative that they would like to send a card to.

2. Help children fold or cut paper into their card shape of choice.

3. Allow space for children to design a card for their chosen person.

4. Ask children to help you address an envelope and send the card in the mail.

SIMPLE SWAP: Instead of sending a card, children can also connect with friends and family via phone or video call. The most important part of this activity is the opportunity for children to reach out to their loved ones and show that they are thinking of them.

MESSINESS:	PREP TIME:	ACTIVITY TIME:	AGE:
2	3 minutes	10 minutes	3 to 4

SANDPAPER OR COTTON

Physically experiencing the difference between pleasant textures and uncomfortable ones can help children make the connection between how kind or unkind words can feel to someone emotionally.

MATERIALS:

COTTON BALLS

PIECE OF SANDPAPER

STEPS:

1. Show your child a handful of cotton balls and let them explore the material. Invite them to talk about what it feels like. Note how soft and fluffy the cotton is.

2. Do the same with a piece of sandpaper. Note the rough texture and sharp feeling on their skin.

3. Ask your child, "If words were cotton balls, what would they feel like? If words were sandpaper, what would they feel like?"

4. Discuss examples of words that would feel like cotton balls and ones that would feel like sandpaper. Ask your child, "Which type of words would you rather hear? What kinds of words do you think other people would like you to say to them?"

GET CREATIVE: Try this activity using different types of materials and textures. Sometimes words can feel cold and uncomfortable like an ice cube or comforting like a warm, soft blanket.

SIMON SAYS

Listening skills play a large part in helping us understand what we can do to help others. Active listening can help children really hear what others need. It also allows them to imagine behaviors that could be helpful in the future.

MATERIALS:

NONE

STEPS:

1. Tell your little one that you are going to play a game called Simon Says. In this game, the caller (Simon) tells the player what to do, and players must complete the action. However, if the caller does not say, "Simon says . . ." before the action, then the players must remain still.

2. If the player moves or completes the action without hearing "Simon says . . ." first, then they receive a strike. Three strikes and they're out!

3. Take turns being the caller and the player.

GET CREATIVE: Try playing this game using emotion words and behaviors. For example, the caller could say, "Simon says . . . act like you're excited/ confused/frustrated," or "Simon says . . . show me a happy smile/an angry stomp."

WE CARE CENTER

This activity provides children with a resource to help them express empathy in a symbolic way, whether that is through creating a get-well card for a friend or providing a family member with a cuddly stuffed animal when they are sad.

MATERIALS:

LARGE BOX

COMFORTING OBJECTS, SUCH AS BANDAGES, STUFFED ANIMALS, AND BLANKETS

CRAFTING SUPPLIES, SUCH AS PAPER OR CARDSTOCK, CONSTRUCTION PAPER, COLORING UTENSILS, MARKERS, GLITTER GLUE, AND STICKERS

STEPS:

1. Explain what a We Care Center is—a place for materials and objects that they can use to help others feel better.

2. Ask your child to help you create a We Care Center for your home or classroom.

3. Together, fill a box with comforting items, such as bandages, stuffed animals, blankets, and crafting supplies. Ask your child what they think should be included in the center and what types of material items or gestures they would appreciate if they were not feeling well physically or emotionally.

4. Invite your child to decorate the box and create a sign to label their center.

AGE ADAPTATION: Enhance your center by providing the option of baking treats for others, gathering flowers from outside, and other activities that require support from older children or adults.

COOKIE DECORATING

Practicing active listening skills, along with asking questions and following directions, can help little ones learn to perceive other's needs.

MATERIALS:

PLAIN PERSON-SHAPED
COOKIES

COOKIE DECORATING
MATERIALS, SUCH
AS ICING, CANDIES,
LICORICE ROPES, ETC.

STEPS:

1. Place one cookie on a flat surface next to the decorating materials.

2. Tell your child that you will be taking turns decorating cookies and that each of you will design a cookie based on the other person's instructions and preferences.

3. Volunteer to decorate first. Begin by asking how they would like their cookie to look and what types of decorations they want you to use. Model active listening skills by asking clarifying questions and instructing your little one to be specific about numbers and placement of decorations.

4. Once you are finished with one cookie, switch roles.

5. Reflect with children on how well you were both able to listen and follow each other's instructions.

SIMPLE SWAP: This activity can also be done with playdough pieces or with paper and crafting materials instead.

TREE OF KINDNESS

Random acts of kindness are just that—small gestures or actions taken to show kindness toward others. Encourage children to grow their trees of kindness!

MATERIALS:

MULTICOLORED CONSTRUCTION PAPER

SCISSORS

TAPE

MARKERS

STEPS:

1. Use construction paper to create a paper tree together—it can be as small or as large as you like. Then cut out heart shapes small enough to tape onto the tree.

2. Talk with children about random acts of kindness and provide examples, such as smiling at someone or letting someone else go first.

3. Invite children to share random acts of kindness they have completed during the past week. If there are none, make suggestions for actions they could complete in the next 10 minutes.

4. Once completed, write down one act of kindness on each heart and have children tape them to their tree.

5. Continue adding hearts as more acts of kindness are completed.

GET CREATIVE: Encourage children to set weekly or monthly goals for their tree.

CHAPTER SIX

The World Is Full of Friends

This chapter is about teaching children empathy and compassion for those who may be different from themselves. Children will also learn how to show respect for all kinds of people. It is often easier to feel empathy for those we feel are most like ourselves, but extending kindness to those who are not like us is just as important. By learning how to show compassion and care to all groups of people in your community, children will build the skills they need to meet everyone with empathy.

ACTIVITY BOXES

This activity can help children imagine what life may be like for people struggling with their health, and understand the need for compassionate support.

MATERIALS:

EMPTY BOXES

DONATIONS, SUCH AS ART SUPPLIES, BLANKETS, AND GAMES

CRAFTING MATERIALS, SUCH AS PAPER OR CARDSTOCK, CONSTRUCTION PAPER, COLORING UTENSILS, MARKERS, GLITTER GLUE, AND STICKERS

STEPS:

1. With your child, create an activity box for kids who are ill and need to stay in the hospital for long periods of time.

2. Discuss what it feels like when they are sick and what types of things are comforting or help them feel better.

3. Fill the box with things your child feels others would want in this situation—art supplies, blankets, games, and any other objects that could help a child pass the time and brighten their day.

4. Decorate the box and a card and/or drawing to go inside. (It will be helpful to research local hospital requirements for donations).

5. Make a special trip with your little one to drop off the box at a hospital's donation center.

GET CREATIVE: If you have the means, consider involving your little one in helping other kids in need. Find a trusted organization that helps provide resources for young people around the world, and donate together with your child, talking about why you are doing so.

WE ARE ALL PEOPLE

When building compassion for others, it is important for children to remember to be kind to everyone, no matter their differences.

MATERIALS:

HANDFUL OF CANDY-COATED CHOCOLATES IN A VARIETY OF COLORS BUT ALL WITH THE SAME CENTER

STEPS:

1. Present your little one with a handful of candies in different colors.

2. Ask children what they notice about how the candies look. Together, note that they are all different colors.

3. Break open each candy to reveal the inside. Point out that even though the candies look different on the outside, they are all the same on the inside.

4. Relate the candies to people—we all may look different on the outside, but on the inside, everyone is a person with their own feelings, wants, and needs.

5. Talk about the importance of treating everyone with equal amounts of kindness no matter what they look like or how different they are from you.

SIMPLE SWAP: Instead of candy, use pictures of different people. Discuss how some people look similar or different, but that on the inside they are all humans.

LEMONADE STAND

Collect donations for a charity!

MATERIALS:

PITCHER

LEMONADE

CUPS

TABLE

JAR

PAPER

MARKER

STEPS:

1. Talk with your child about what a charity is and how they help different groups of people. Ask them if they would like to raise money for a charity and what group of people or cause they want to assist.

2. Suggest a lemonade stand. Make a pitcher of lemonade and help your child set up shop on the sidewalk or in a park. Work with your little one to create a sign for their stand as well as a jar for donations.

3. For the next few hours, allow your child to take the lead running the stand, giving away cups of lemonade in exchange for donations. Encourage them to discuss their chosen cause with patrons.

4. After the sales are complete, help your child count out the donation total and praise them for their hard work.

5. Share the donation with the chosen charity and ask your child how this experience made them feel.

SIMPLE SWAP: Whip up a batch of cookies or brownies with your little one and have a bake sale instead!

CEREAL BIRD FEEDER

Taking care of animals can promote empathy in children by allowing them to experience what it feels like to support and consider the needs of another being.

MATERIALS:

CIRCLE-SHAPED CEREAL

PIPE CLEANERS

STEPS:

1. Show children how to thread cereal onto a pipe cleaner until it is almost completely covered. (For animal safety, be sure to use whole-grain cereal without added sugars or dyes!)

2. Take both ends of the pipe cleaner and twist them together so that they connect. Allow children to bend the pipe cleaner into any shape they like.

3. Hang the feeders on the branch of a tree or bush outside and enjoy watching birds stop by for a snack.

4. Ask children how it feels to help take care of the birds and provide them with food.

GET CREATIVE: Encourage children to help you take care of pets at home or accompany children in volunteering at a local animal shelter. These actions can help build a sense of responsibility and pride in children.

VISITING OLDER ADULTS

Give children the opportunity to make a new friend from another generation. Allow them to build their interpersonal skills while also promoting empathy toward the elderly population.

MATERIALS:

NONE

STEPS:

1. After calling ahead to inquire about visiting guidelines and rules, take about 30 minutes to visit a local nursing home or senior center.

2. Encourage children to interact with the residents and ask them questions about their lives or play games with them.

3. Invite children to return weekly or monthly. Talk about what it would be like to live in a nursing home. Discuss with children how they think their visits may impact the people they have been spending time with.

AGE ADAPTATION: For younger ones, invite children to create decorations for a local nursing home—pictures for the walls or banners to celebrate birthdays. Talk with children about what they would like to see on the walls if they lived there.

PARK CLEANUP

Pick up litter in a community space!

MATERIALS:

PLASTIC BAGS

DISPOSABLE GLOVES

STEPS:

1. Go to a community park with your children and take a few minutes to talk about things that they notice. Ask them how the people in the park are enjoying themselves and if the park looks safe and clean.

2. Invite the children to discuss how litter in the park could affect the people and animals trying to enjoy it.

3. Take a short walk. Have both you and the children put on disposable gloves, and encourage them to help you pick up any litter that you see.

4. After disposing of the trash properly, ask the children, "How does it feel to pick up litter that is not yours? Do you think cleaning the park made a difference for the people and animals using it? Would you want others to keep a park clean that you were playing in?"

SIMPLE SWAP: This activity can also be completed in a neighboring community. Talk with children about what it is like to clean a space that they do not typically use and how it feels to help others.

RESOURCES

Websites

Emotions chart: HappierHuman.com/wp-content/uploads/2021/04/teacherspayteachers.jpg

Harvard's Making Caring Common Project: "5 Tips for Cultivating Empathy": MCC.GSE.Harvard.edu/resources-for-families/5-tips-cultivating-empathy

This helpful article provides in-depth suggestions for caregivers as well as a number of tips to encourage participation and empathetic skill-building in children.

Reversible figures: ResearchGate.net/profile/John-Gero/publication/236867167/figure/fig1/AS:799066531299330@1567523715728/Four-reversible-figures-the-duck-rabbit-the-hawk-goose-the-snail-elephant-and-the.png

Scholastic: "Age-by-Age Advice for Teaching Empathy": Scholastic.com/parents/family-life/parent-child/age-age-advice-teaching-empathy.html

This resource offers best practice recommendations to help caregivers teach empathy and compassion to children of all ages.

Zero to Three: "How to Help Your Child Develop Empathy": ZeroToThree.org/resources/5-how-to-help-your-child-develop-empathy

This early childhood website provides developmental milestones in empathy and tips for caregivers to help foster empathetic skills.

Books

The Everything Parent's Guide to Emotional Intelligence in Children: How to Raise Children Who Are Caring, Resilient, and Emotionally Strong
by Korrel Kanoy, PhD
This book presents a deep dive into how to promote emotional intelligence in children.

Simple Acts: The Busy Family's Guide to Giving Back
by Natalie Silverstein, MPH
This book provides parents with practical ideas to involve the whole family in helping others in the community.

UnSelfie: Why Empathetic Kids Succeed in Our All-About-Me World
by Michele Borba, EdD
This book offers a guide for caregivers to learn more about social patterns in youth today and suggestions for how to help children build empathy.

REFERENCES

Goleman, Daniel. *Emotional Intelligence*. New York: Bantam, 1995.

Murray, Desiree W., Katie Rosanbalm, Christina Christopoulos, and Amar Hamoudi. *Self-Regulation and Toxic Stress: Foundations for Understanding Self-Regulation from an Applied Developmental Perspective*. OPRE Report #2015–21 (Washington, DC: Office of Planning, Research and Evaluation, Administration for Children and Families, US Department of Health and Human Services, 2015).

INDEX

Acknowledgments

This book could not have been written without the love and support from my family and friends. Thank you for your continued confidence and encouragement. You are so appreciated!

About the Author

 **NICOLE TOLENTINO** is a licensed clinical social worker in Chicago, Illinois, and has devoted much of her career to working with young people as a school social worker and social-emotional learning specialist. She earned her bachelor's degree in early childhood education at Indiana University and later went on to obtain her master's degree in social work from the University of Illinois.